MW00935250

The guidance given in this book relates solely to general astrological
considerations. For detailed advice regarding your personal situation,
consult a qualified professional practitioner in the relevant field.

YOUR HOROSCOPE 2020

CAPRICORN

ZOE BUCKDEN

General Trends

The main trend this year is stability. After the upheaval of the last two years, as Uranus moved from Aries to Taurus, everything has settled into a new pattern. That doesn't mean life will be dull! Uranus brings radical change to our lives, and is now busy overhauling your solar house of love. This covers romance and love affairs, but also creative projects, children and child-figures (such as anyone you mentor or provide care for), and anything you're passionate about. Leisure activities, sports, and hobbies also fall under the same house.

Everything that brings you joy will be energised by the electric energy of this unpredictable planet. The process will continue for several more years, so don't get too comfortable!

If there are young children in your life, keep a very close eye on them. Uranus energy is exuberant, rebellious, and erratic. Accidents and injuries are likely. Make sure you take all sensible precautions.

That said, what we do have this year is an anchor. Realistic Saturn is spending one last year in Capricorn, your own sun sign and solar house of self. This brings order to the chaos. You will feel this more strongly than any other sun sign, since Saturn is your personal ruler and you are uniquely attuned to its level-headed energy.

On the flip side, Saturn forces us to deal with things as they are, rather than as we wish them to be. If anything in your life rests on shaky ground, the shifting sands may cause the whole edifice to crash down. Flaws and problems can no longer be concealed. It will not be possible to hide from the truth. Saturn will show you what needs to be done to get your life firmly on the right track. This may feel overwhelming at times, but is always to your benefit. Stay strong!

Powerful Pluto, ruler of your friendship house, is standing close by to lend its support. You are uniquely privileged to have two such champions in your corner! And this year you get another fabulous bonus. Jupiter, the Great Protector, is travelling through your own sun sign of Capricorn for the entire year, leaving in late December. This will shield you from harm, and expand your life in all the areas you treasure most.

As if that weren't enough, idealistic Neptune in visionary Pisces, the sign of dreams and wishes, sends its blessing throughout the year. This is a time to release the parts of your life that don't actually matter to you deep down, and nurture those that do. Allow the process to happen. You will emerge from it freshly cleansed, with a clear sense of honest purpose and the insight to make your dreams come true.

The times when you will come face to face with your own personal challenges are the start of the year and the weeks around midsummer. This is because the Cancer-Capricorn eclipse series that began last year continues with further eclipses during those periods. Expect major events and shattering revelations at these times. The series ends with a lunar eclipse in Capricorn in early July, which concludes the transformation of your houses of self and relationships. There will be no further eclipses along this axis until 2027. Whatever the situation is at the end of summer, that's the reality from now on.

Such times can be difficult to deal with. We are all fallible, and on occasion cling to false hopes and illusions. Expect to discover truths you would prefer not to have known. Remember that ignorance isn't bliss, it's just blinkers. You can only choose the best path forward if you know where you stand.

That said, all the eclipses are benign. Even if you experience disappointment, you will soon recognise the upside. Perhaps you'll get confirmation of what you've suspected for a while, or have the relief of finally being able to do what you know in your heart is right. There is nothing to fear from these eclipses, and much to gain from the revelations they bring.

Also this year we have a new eclipse series on the Gemini-Sagittarius axis, which will transform your houses of inner needs and outer health, what you want and how you go about achieving it. The series opens in June, just as the Cancer-Capricorn series is ending, so the summer months will be full of drama. Plan to do as little as possible during this unsettled time.

The Gemini-Sagittarius series continues through the winter, and runs until the end of next year, so you'll have plenty of time to adjust to the news it brings. With Neptune in difficult angle, these eclipses may be hard on your feelings, and you may experience a lot of confusion and bewilderment. Don't try to make sense of anything straight away. Allow matters to develop fully. You probably won't know the real truth until the series has ended, so take no action unless it's absolutely necessary. Sit back and watch the situation unfold.

It's always best not to initiate anything during an eclipse, because circumstances are changing fast and you don't yet know how things will shake out. That's especially true this year. It's fine to respond when appropriate, but don't try to start anything yourself. Just let the universe speak.

You may notice the effects of an eclipse exactly one month before or after the date of the eclipse itself. Watch for significant events at these times.

Adding to the unsettled atmosphere, Venus is retrograde in Gemini during early summer. Since Venus is the planet of love and harmony, this would usually suggest people problems, but aspects are good and there won't be any serious disagreements. Miscommunication and misunderstandings are more likely, and there could be a general air of confusion. With your ruler Saturn also retrograde and in benevolent angle, issues from the past are likely to surface and come to a happy resolution – eventually. This could take a while, so don't expect rapid progress. Above all, don't push. Listen more than you speak. Allow matters to reach their own natural conclusion.

There won't be much scope for action during the rest of the year, as all the outer planets are retrograde in late summer and energy planet Mars is retrograde in its own sign of Aries during the autumn. Long-term projects may stall, and new ventures blow up in unexpected ways. It's best to leave things be.

Frustration will be rife as fiery Mars clashes with powerful Pluto and stern Saturn. Expect major roadblocks, immovable obstacles, and fierce power struggles throughout the autumn months. You will feel this most strongly in your personal and domestic life, but your friends and social circle (including any groups, clubs, and organisations you belong to) may be affected as well.

Do as little as possible. Stand your ground if you must, but don't force a confrontation. Be careful in safety matters. Avoid taking risks.

Since the second half of the year will be criss-crossed with difficult energies, it's best not to start anything important then. If you have projects that you're keen to get off the ground, launch them early in the year. Powerful new moons during the first few months offer diamond-studded opportunities. Nail down your plans well in advance, and act promptly when the moment comes. You will be rewarded with great success!

Your birthday month this year will be full of fizz. The mighty Sun in your own sign, with electrifying Uranus in happy angle in your house of love, brings fabulous energy to your life.

Adventure and opportunity will open up before you, and anything that's been holding you back will disappear. Embrace your freedom!

If you have important projects to launch, a gorgeous new moon in mid-January 2021 will provide a fantastic opening.

Spend the intervening time marshalling your resources and nailing down your plans and preparations.

The most stable areas of your life this year will be career, travel and learning, and shared property and inheritance (including childhood issues and emotional "baggage" of all kinds). No major changes are due, so enjoy things as they are.

January

The new year gets off to a fantastic start, with amazing harmony between all the planets. Lots of happy aspects bring the party atmosphere to New Year's Day. A cluster of five joyful planets celebrate together in your very own sun sign of Capricorn, which means everything you do will buzz with happy energy. You're still in last year's birthday month, so this is the perfect time to set things in motion.

Act in the first few days of the new year if you can. There's still plenty of new moon energy from the solar eclipse a few days ago, which will give all your projects a fabulous push. After the first week has passed, it's best not to launch anything major. Another eclipse is looming, and although it's very positive, it will swirl things around. Launch crucial ventures straight away, or else wait until a more settled time.

Three of the planets in Capricorn are communing with erratic Uranus, planet of change, which is retrograde in your house of love (which covers romance and children, but also creative projects and anything you're passionate about). This means there's strong but unpredictable backward-looking energy fizzing around. Focus on existing plans and projects if you can. Past work may bring unexpected rewards.

Flashes of insight, strokes of luck, and all sorts of unexpected events are on the cards. Don't fight it. Just let it happen. You'll get to see the benefits later on.

It's a perfect time to enjoy the company of your loved ones. If you're single and looking, an exciting prospect (possibly an old flame) may appear in your life. Have fun, but don't expect things to last. Uranus energy is liberating rather than reliable. This should be a happy and adventurous time, so enjoy the ride! Just don't make any long-term plans. Allow the situation to unfold at its own pace.

It's also an intuitive time, with the Moon close to Neptune in visionary Pisces. You could well have profound breakthroughs, whether practical or spiritual. The road ahead could become clear, and you may realise just how to turn your dreams into reality. Give your conscious and unconscious mind free rein, brainstorm solutions, let inspiration come.

There is a strong emphasis on the elements of earth and water, with every planet except Venus in an earth or water sign. Get outdoors if you can. Commune with nature. The practical and the spiritual work together right now, so take a break if you need it and allow body and soul to reconnect.

It's a time for preparation, rather than action. If you have projects to launch and plans to set in motion, do so at the end of the month, when a splendid new moon will give you all the support you could hope for. Right now, simply get your ducks in a row, and wait.

On Friday 3 Mars leaves water sign Scorpio and moves into fire sign Sagittarius, your house of inner needs. With Jupiter, the ruler of Sagittarius, in splendid angle to retrograde Uranus, this is a good time to act if you must, provided you are implementing existing plans or retreading familiar ground. Don't do anything completely new.

Act promptly, though, because the next eclipse is almost upon us. Friday 3 through Monday 6 are suitable, but after that do as little as possible. There is simply too much static in the air.

On Friday 10 a full moon lunar eclipse in Cancer brings something to an end in your relationship house. This follows on from the eclipse in Capricorn in late December and continues the Cancer-Capricorn series that began with a new moon solar eclipse in Cancer in mid-July 2018. By now you may have an idea of how this series will transform your life in the areas of self and relationships, who you are and how that reflects back at you through your most important connections. If not, don't worry. All will become clear in time.

The current eclipse is benign but extremely powerful. Saturn, your personal ruler, is meeting with life-changing Pluto in your very own sun sign of Capricorn. This fateful encounter will bring a massive shift in everyone's lives, through social forces beyond our individual control, but you will feel it more strongly than any other sign. Both planets are closely involved with the eclipse, so the effects will be felt immediately although the full repercussions will take years to process. Tread with care.

Idealistic Neptune in friendly angle shows that the best thing to do is hold fast to your highest self. Keep your own true values firmly before you, and act in accordance with them. Don't initiate anything at all, but do respond to events if you honestly believe it's the right thing to do.

Two days later, on Sunday 12, Uranus turns direct in your house of love after having been retrograde since mid-August last year. This throws an element of the unpredictable into the mix. Kind beams from Jupiter and Venus will soothe and enhance the effects, so good things are coming. But the ride may prove bumpy, so keep your seatbelt fastened.

At mid-month the Sun leaves your own sun sign of Capricorn to enter Aquarius, shifting the emphasis from your house of self to your house of money and personal resources. Communicative Mercury, travelling alongside the mighty Sun, could bring news. You may not like what you hear. Uranus, the ruler of Áquarius, is in hard angle and still frazzled from its change of direction. Don't act on the news just yet. Wait until Sunday 26 or the days immediately after, when Mercury will have lovely aspects and be able to support you.

On Friday 24 a new moon in Aquarius brings a fresh start to this same house of money and personal resources. Grouchy

Uranus in difficult angle will throw a spanner in the works, so expect the unexpected. If you have projects to get off the ground, don't act at once. Wait until Sunday 26 when the Moon and Uranus are friends again. Aspects will be lovely then, so do put your plans in motion.

Don't delay! From the end of the month you may begin to feel the effects of Mercury's impending retrograde in Pisces, your house of everyday routines, in mid-February. Since Mercury is the planet of travel and communication, these areas hit snags whenever the planet changes direction. Traffic jams, payment glitches, equipment failures, delays and frustration are all likely. Get things sorted now, then leave all such matters alone until Mercury is back in business at the end of March.

The outlook continues stormy for another reason, too. Uranus, planet of radical change, will be at loggerheads with realistic Saturn from now until June. Conditions that no longer serve your needs, especially regarding people and projects that matter to you personally, will begin to collapse. Accept the necessity of growth, even if it's daunting. Release all that is rigid and stultifying, and set yourself free. If you feel held back by forces beyond your control, look for ways to make gradual changes. The most important thing is to allow growth to happen. Don't cling to the apparent safety of a rut.

A word of caution. These are powerful planets, and both in earth signs. As when tension builds up along the edges of tectonic plates, then is released all at once in a massive earthquake, so the shift when it finally comes could be catastrophic. Clear the decks if you can. Check your money and housing situation. Beware of anything that may be built on sand. Financial or property crashes are possible. If natural disasters are a threat where you live, take steps to keep yourself and your loved ones safe.

But do have faith. Benevolent Jupiter and high-minded Neptune are deep in conversation, and will do all they can to help. Messages of hope will arrive throughout the spring. This is a time of opportunity, if you remain open to the possibility of change.

February

This month is all about Pisces, sign of dreams and wishes, your house of everyday routines (including your neighbourhood and workplace, and your ordinary environment in general). Since 2012 this sign has been strengthened by the presence of its ruler, idealistic Neptune, which brings visionary insight to your day-to-day life.

Even the seemingly humdrum can be a source of spiritual revelation. With Neptune as your guide, you are able to see extraordinary truths within your ordinary surroundings.

Neptune will move on in 2025, so you have plenty of time to benefit from its presence. But this month the effect will be heightened by a cavalcade of happy planets passing through Pisces, each in turn receiving the blessing of mighty Neptune.

You will discover great joy and a higher meaning in all that you do. Harmony planet Venus is already in Pisces as the month opens, adding beams of earthly love to the heavenly rays of Neptune. This wonderful energy lasts only for one final week before Venus moves into Aries, your house of home and family, on Saturday 8.

Around the same time, during the days surrounding Monday 10, you may feel the effects of last month's eclipse in Cancer, your relationship house. Because Cancer is a water sign like Pisces, the two have a natural affinity with each other. If you didn't receive a message under the January eclipse, you may well hear it now.

The upshot is that any day-to-day matters you want to bring to a conclusion is what you should prioritise at the beginning of the month.

Don't start anything new. A full moon is looming, which means this is a time of fulfilment and conclusion.

Whatever you've been working on, especially anything that began under the new moon and solar eclipse in Cancer in early July last year, or anything that began under the new moon in Leo (your house of shared property and inheritance, including childhood issues and emotional "baggage" of all kinds) in early August, is ripe for completion now.

On Sunday 9 a full moon in Leo brings something to an end in your house of shared property and inheritance. This is a positive full moon, with energy planet Mars in happy angle in your house of inner needs. Lovely angles throughout the chart, especially in the personal area, offer the chance to bring projects to a satisfying conclusion. Take care to dot all the i's and cross the t's, though, as Mercury's impending retrograde could bring gremlins out to play!

Echoes of last month's eclipse in Cancer may reverberate at this time, so tread with care. Stay true to your core values, and seek the highest good. Don't be misled by false appearances or wishful thinking. You may discover new solutions to old problems, or hear about further developments in a matter you thought had been settled. If so, the real conclusion may not come until mid-March. Stay tuned.

On Tuesday 18 February Mercury turns retrograde in Pisces, your house of everyday routines. As always, expect plenty of static in the days surrounding the planet's change of direction. Mercury rules travel and communication, so there will be plenty of glitches in this area. Expect delays, confusion, misunderstandings, and low-key frazzle of all kinds. With dreamy Neptune nearby, it may be difficult to get straight answers to the simplest of questions. Don't try to resolve anything complicated. Just accept that it will take time to straighten things out.

This is an excellent time to slow down and triple check everything you do. Make sure your processes are as foolproof as you can make them. In the next few weeks, use Mercury's retrograde energy to review, re-think, and re-visit projects rather than press ahead with anything new.

Stress and illness are possible, since Mercury rules your house of health. The same house also cover work, in the sense of all the practical steps you take to turn your dreams into reality, so expect plenty of obstacles, snags and frustration. This can be tough to deal with, but use it as an opportunity to review, re-think, and re-consider. Retrograde energy is backwards-looking, so anything that involves covering familiar ground will shine right now. Consolidate the work you've done so far, rather than attempt to press forward.

20

On Wednesday 20 the Sun moves into Pisces, bringing extra emphasis to your house of everyday routines. With Mercury moving backwards through this sign, you'll have plenty of opportunity to consider where you stand. You may get some wonderful news.

If you want to take action, do so on or after Sunday 23 when a gorgeous new moon lights up this same area of everyday routines. Act on well-established plans or projects already underway. It's a fantastic opportunity to give things an extra push. Mars in Capricorn and Uranus in Taurus send powerful energy, enough to move mountains. These are forceful planets, so expect earth-shaking results. Mercury retrograde near the Moon brings a message from the past, and a reminder to get every detail right. This could be a splendid opportunity to regroup and try again, and finally set things on the right track.

Get everything done and dusted in the days immediately following the new moon. The last few days of February are likely to be frustrating and emotional. Harmony planet Venus in uncongenial Aries gets an earful from a cluster of domineering planets in your own sign, no-nonsense Capricorn, while the sensitive Moon nearby brings a risk of hurt feelings and unnecessary drama. Be tactful with other people, especially family and loved ones, even if they're in the wrong. We are all human! Tread gently, and wait for the atmosphere to settle. From mid-March onwards, the clouds will scatter and the sun shine through once again.

March

The headline news this month is that Saturn, the Great Teacher, changes sign. After travelling through its home sign of Capricorn since 2017, the planet is ready to move on.

You will have felt the effects of Saturn's presence more strongly than anyone else, since the planet is your personal ruler and is at its strongest in your own sun sign. The past few years have been a time of testing, where flaws become apparent and difficulties mount.

This won't have been easy. Saturn teaches by showing us what's wrong, so that we can fix it. Many things will have gone awry.

The good news is that you are uniquely attuned to this planet's energy, and so best placed of all the signs to make the most of the knowledge it brings.

Hopefully you are now in a place where your life is stronger and better for Saturn's tuition. If not, rest assured that you soon will be. Saturn's lessons are costly, but well worth the price.

From now on, things may seem to get easier. Don't relax just yet! Saturn will retrograde back into Capricorn in early July and remain there until the end of the year. Issues you thought had been dealt with and situations that seemed to have resolved may flare up again. Your own fixes may prove to be inadequate. This is a chance to re-visit problems and make sure the solutions are rock solid. Take the time to work through each issue from the ground up. Saturn won't return to your own sun sign for many years, so it's worth getting everything straightened out now.

This month may feel like the crunch point. With stern Saturn in hard angle to rebellious Uranus, tensions are running high. Mercury retrograde will bring up issues from the past. It's a good time to look back and try to understand what the real problem is. Review, re-think, and re-visit, but don't push for instant solutions. The situation may be more complex than it appears. Full resolution is unlikely until later in the year.

On Friday 6 Mercury retrogrades into Aquarius, your money house, which is ruled by Uranus. On the same day, Venus moves into Taurus, your house of love, which it rules. The week that follows will fizz and sparkle with electric energy. Venus in close support of Uranus, and Mercury in happy angle to them both, gives an extra boost to the rebel cause. This could be the time when bonds shatter and rigid structures come tumbling down.

Be careful. Freedom is a splendid thing, but when the walls crumble we must take care not to be hit by falling masonry. Mercury's turn direct on Tuesday 10 will add plenty of static to the already frazzled atmosphere. Don't do anything in haste.

That said, most of the chart is full of happy aspects. Only Saturn in your house of self insists on throwing a wet blanket over the party atmosphere. Treat this venerable planet with respect, like a grumpy old neighbour who demands that the music be turned down. Saturn is on the brink of leaving its home in your own sun sign of Capricorn, and set out on a long journey around the rest of the zodiac wheel. Even a wise and ancient planet may need a little compassion at such a time. Be gracious, and you will reap the rewards.

On Monday 9 a full moon in Virgo brings something to an end in your house of travel and learning (the "travel" of the mind). Since Virgo is ruled by Mercury, you may experience glitches and delays due to the planet's change of direction. It's a good time to finish up projects, but don't expect things to run smoothly. Dreamy Neptune in opposition close to the Sun could add a layer of confusion and wishful thinking. Triple-check everything, and nail down every detail.

It's not a great time to sign contracts, but if you must do so, a cluster of happy planets will help keep things positive. Just don't expect this to be the final word. Further developments are likely. A glorious new moon in late April provides the opportunity to set things on a better footing, and if you can wait until early September, a full moon in Pisces offers beautiful aspects in support of a harmonious agreement. Delay until then if you can.

On Monday 16 Mercury re-enters Pisces, bringing news or insights regarding everyday matters. Uranus and the Moon add their input from your houses of love and inner needs. Relationships with your loved ones will sparkle, and creative projects fizz with inspiration. New solutions to old problems may occur to you. If so, the new moon later in the month could provide the perfect opportunity to implement them. Make your plans now!

The next few days are ideal for ordinary matters or anything close to home. With the Sun, Neptune, and Mercury all in your house of everyday routines and in beautiful aspects to other planets, this is a lovely time to reflect on what you want from life. It's also a chance to tidy up any loose ends left over from the full moon. Anything that got delayed or stirred up by the static surrounding Mercury's change of direction can be put to bed now without any fuss.

On Friday 20 the Sun moves into Aries, and the new zodiac year begins. With happy angles to Pluto and Saturn in your own sign of Capricorn, this sets the stage for a successful launch of long-term projects. Set your plans in motion on or after the new moon in Aries on Tuesday 24 as this will get you off to the perfect start.

Anything connected with money, home, and family is especially blessed right now. But whatever your goals, this gorgeous new moon will help you achieve them.

The most sensational event of the month, Saturn's move from Capricorn into Aquarius, takes place on Sunday 22, just before the new moon arrives. This will bring a flurry of activity during the weeks surrounding this date. You may notice these signals from mid-month onwards, but the new moon will bring them into sharp focus.

Although Saturn usually turns up difficulties, right now a cluster of enthusiastic supporting planets is giving Saturn a fabulous send-off from its home sign. This is more likely to bring rewards than reproaches. Late March could be a splendid time, when the benefits of Saturn's three-year journey through your house of self become clear. You are the star of the zodiac right now. Enjoy!

April

This month the planetary emphasis shifts to your house of money and personal resources. Saturn, the Great Teacher, is now moving through this house and will spend the next few years helping you put everything in order.

You'll get off to a dramatic start. Energy planet Mars moved into Aquarius alongside Saturn right at the end of last month, so the two planets are travelling together throughout the first half of April.

This can be tough on everyone, because the two don't make ideal companions. The fiery aggression of Mars is at odds with the slow cold calculation of Saturn. Erratic Uranus in hard angle won't improve matters either. Expect fireworks as the month opens.

If changes are necessary in your life, this may become apparent now. Frustration, anger, and resentment may boil over, or long-standing conflicts erupt into sudden rows. Clear the air if necessary, but be careful not to let things to spiral out of control. Avoid risky activities.

It's an excellent time to sort out anything that needs dealing with, if you are sure of what you want to do. If not, throw yourself into constructive and practical work. There's lots of energy available, so use it for good if you can. Seek professional advice regarding any legal or financial issues that arise.

Harmony planet Venus, secure in its home sign of Taurus, sends its blessings, so peace and concord are possible. Although Venus moves into Gemini on Saturday 4, the loving rays continue. Solutions may emerge once the situation has been clarified.

On Wednesday 8 a full moon in Libra brings something to an end in your career house. Jupiter and Pluto in hard angle suggest ego conflicts and power struggles. Some kind of confrontation seems likely. It's still a good time to finish things, but be diplomatic if you can. Neptune and Mercury send messages of calm and reason, so a compromise may be possible. Strive to see the other person's point of view.

On Sunday 19 the Sun enters Taurus, your house of love. This gives a boost to rebellious Uranus in its long-running battle with Saturn. With Jupiter and Pluto also joining the fray, there's tremendous tension in the air. Venus has moved out of harm's way to let the combatants sort things out for themselves.

Everyone will feel this tension. For you, a conflict between love and practicality seems most likely. There may not be a solution right now, as no other planets are involved.

The new moon in Taurus on Thursday 23 lands on the Uranus side of the deadlock. This brings a new beginning in your house of love, but at great cost. With the Sun, the Moon, and Uranus all pulling in the same direction, and with fresh new-moon energy to point the way, change can no longer be resisted. But Pluto, Saturn, and Jupiter are doing their best to block it, and with all the backwards pull of their own impending retrogrades on their side.

It's a fraught situation. This is make-or-break time, and fractures are likely. Take care. Powerful forces are in play. If you want to start something new, especially in the areas of finance, romance, or creative pursuits, by all means do so but be aware you'll run into strong opposition. Even if you get your way now, there are roadblocks ahead. Make sure you know what you're doing.

Conversely, if you're resisting change, recognise that it'll win out in the end. Much as we might wish to hold on to the past, once it's gone there's no going back. By all means pause to consider the full impact of any new developments, but do accept that the existing situation can't last. Something has to crack. Make sure it isn't you.

On Monday 27, communicative Mercury enters Taurus to join the support that clusters around Uranus. This could bring the glimmer of an answer. The Moon in helpful angle in sensitive Cancer, your relationship house, suggests that emotional intelligence is key to finding a solution that works for everyone. Stay at the negotiating table, and keep an open mind. Good news may arrive as early as next month, although complete resolution isn't likely until late autumn.

During these last few days of the month, you may begin to feel the effects of Venus' impending retrograde in Gemini, your house of health and work. Since Venus is the planet of love, this could affect personal relationships and make everyone a little more irritable than usual. You'll feel this more strongly than most, since Venus also rules your solar house of love (including romance and children). But with the sympathetic Moon and forceful Mars both offering support, the effects are likely to be mild. Harmonious relations are possible, with a bit of goodwill on all sides.

May

This month is all about the Venus retrograde in Gemini, your house of health and work. You will feel the effects throughout the next few months. Romance, children, creative projects, and professional matters may also be affected, since your houses of love and career are ruled by Venus.

Where loved ones are concerned, you could run into very strong opposition. Mercury and Uranus together in your house of love bring clarity about what needs to change, but stubborn Saturn (your personal ruling planet) in hard angle and Venus slowing down means everything is held back.

Use this time for reflection. Make sure you've considered all reasonable objections. Check for flaws and weaknesses in your arguments or in your plans. Don't press ahead regardless, as you're likely to overlook a significant point. Full resolution won't happen until late autumn in any case, when a full moon in Taurus brings matters to a conclusion.

Consider all the angles. You have plenty of time.

On Thursday 7 a full moon in Scorpio, your house of friendship (including any groups, clubs, and organisations you belong to), brings something to an end in the social sphere. With the mighty Sun, rebellious Uranus, and communicative Mercury all clustered together in direct opposition, conflict is likely.

This will be constructive rather than destructive, though. Protective Jupiter, powerful Pluto, and idealistic Neptune all send their blessings. With so much support, a happy outcome seems assured.

Since this full moon falls on the opposite side of the zodiac wheel to your house of love, whatever ends now may clear the way for a solution to your difficulties in that house. Pluto retrograde suggests the answer may lie in the past, so draw on existing connections and relevant experience.

Also around this time you may feel the effects of next month's eclipse in your house of inner needs. With Jupiter, the ruler of that house, on friendly terms with Pluto, these will be completely benign. Major changes are likely, either now or next month, but they will work in your favour. Good things are coming!

On Monday 11 Mercury enters Gemini, your house of health and work, which it rules. On the same day, your own ruling planet Saturn turns retrograde in your money house. With the two planets in happy angle to each other, you may get news or insights that throw light on a matter from the past. A cluster of planets in your own sun sign and house of self add their input, so news or other developments that closely concern you seem more than likely.

On Wednesday 13 Venus turns retrograde in your house of health and work. With ruler Mercury moving direct in the same house, the two planets will cross paths in the next couple of weeks. You may meet or hear from someone in your past, or possibly experience the resurgence of a health concern. Neptune in hard angle suggests a tussle between idealism and earthly reality. Take care to think clearly. Don't be swept away by your imagination.

At mid-month Jupiter turns retrograde in your own sun sign of Capricorn, which will slow things down in your house of self for the next few months. Since Jupiter rules your house of inner needs, you will notice the slowdown more than most. It may seem impossible to get anywhere with anything. Take the opportunity to review your situation, your aims in life, and your plans for the future. It's a time for reflection, rather than for action.

This is the beginning of a general flow of backwards-looking energy, as nearly all the outer planets will be retrograde during the summer. Only Uranus will continue to move forward. Expect enlightenment, but not much progress, especially regarding personal concerns.

On Wednesday 20 the Sun moves into Gemini, bringing much-needed energy to your house of health and work. Two days later, on Friday 22, a new moon in the same sign brings a fresh start to this house. Lovely support from the retrograde outer planets in Capricorn and Aquarius suggest a joyful new development of an old situation. If you've been struggling with stalled projects, try a fresh approach. It's also a good time to act on plans you've already made. Don't expect rapid progress, but do have faith that the results will come in time.

Also on this day, Friday 22, Mercury and retrograde Venus meet in Gemini. This is the perfect time to re-evaluate an existing situation, or a project that's hit a snag, and decide whether or not to try again. Clear-sighted Mercury will show the way. The effects will be strongest in your house of health and work, but matters concerning your loved ones may be affected as well.

If your life is in good order, the days surrounding this date are ideal for enjoying the company of those you love, meeting friends, or visiting much-loved places. Take a holiday! You've earned it.

June

This month is all about eclipses. In the very first week, on Friday 5 June, a full moon lunar eclipse in Sagittarius brings something to an end in your house of inner needs. This is the first in a new series of eclipses on the Gemini-Sagittarius axis, which will bring dramatic changes to your houses of inner needs and outer health, what you want and how you go about achieving it, during the next two years.

The opening eclipse is friendly, but may not feel much like it. Energy planet Mars in hard angle, and retrograde Venus close to the Sun in direct opposition to the sensitive Moon, makes for a frustrating and difficult time. Feelings may run high. Stress and illness are likely, so take good care of yourself.

But there's also positive news. High-minded Neptune close to Mars brings a wider perspective, supported by happy rays from Jupiter and Pluto in your own sign of Capricorn.

Whatever comes to light now is to your benefit. Listen with an open mind.

It's always best not to take action under an eclipse. Circumstances are changing rapidly, and you don't yet know what the outcome will be. This is especially true right now. With a lot of retrograde energy in play, it's best not to start anything at all. Don't make any important decisions, either. It's fine to respond if necessary, but don't initiate. Allow things to come to their own natural conclusion.

There's a strong air of finality about this eclipse. Jupiter, Pluto, and Neptune will also be involved with next month's eclipse in your own sun sign, which ends the Cancer-Capricorn series that has transformed your houses of self and relationships throughout the past two years. You may feel the effects of that eclipse also around this time.

Overall, the first week in June is a time of endings. Accept the reality, and let go of what is no longer right for you. Only by clearing away the past can you move forward into a bright new future.

For the next two weeks you may feel the effects of

Mercury's impending retrograde in Cancer, your relationship house. Mercury rules travel and communication, so its retrogrades bring delays, snags, and misunderstandings of all kinds. Lovely angles to Mars and Uranus provide electrifying energy, so things may be in even more of a swirl than usual.

It's not a great time to press ahead with anything important, especially if other people are involved, but do take the opportunity to go back over projects and issues from the past. This is a time to review, sort through, fix, and improve anything that hasn't worked out or that you're not entirely happy with.

Don't make any major decisions or agreements, especially regarding relationships (whether personal or professional), as the impending eclipse in that house will shake things up very soon. Stay low-key.

Mercury changes direction on Thursday 18, so expect a lot of static on that day. You will feel this mostly in the area of important relationships, but all areas of your life may be affected. Be patient with the world. It will soon right itself again.

On Sunday 21 the Sun enters Cancer, energising your relationship house even further. On the very same day, a new moon solar eclipse marks a new beginning in that same house of relationships. This is the next to last eclipse in the Cancer-Capricorn series. The final eclipse arrives early next month in own sun sign of Capricorn. After that, we are done with upheaval on this axis until the next series begins in 2027.

The current eclipse is a difficult one. Mars in hard angle brings aggression and conflict, while retrograde Mercury builds frustration. The Moon is at its strongest in Cancer, so emotions will run high. Take care. Accidents, injuries, and illness are all possible. Be mindful of safety. Avoid risk.

Three outer planets are also retrograde, with another about to turn. Progress on all fronts may grind to a halt. This won't make anyone happy, so allow for human frailty and be patient with yourself and others.

Everyone will struggle with this eclipse. You are not alone! Accept that nothing is likely to go smoothly right now. Do good work where you can, speak softly and tread with care, and see what the universe brings.

The end of the month will be chaotic. With the effects of this difficult eclipse still reverberating around the zodiac wheel, Mars enters its own home sign of Aries, where it is strongest. Harmony planet Venus changes direction around the same time, creating further static. Expect conflicts, drama, and angry feelings. These energies could erupt as injuries or ill health, so do stay safe and keep a watchful eye on any children in your life.

On the plus side, there are truly lovely aspects among most of the planets. Peace and goodwill are definitely possible. Conflicts are likely to prove constructive rather than destructive, so assume the best and look for common ground. Sometimes it's necessary to clear the air, so that relationships can flourish on an honest footing. Approach every altercation with an open mind.

Right at the very end of the month, on Tuesday 30, Jupiter and Pluto meet in Capricorn, your own sun sign and solar house of self. This brings the chance for great things. Think deeply about who you are and what you seek to accomplish. Idealistic Neptune in beautiful angle will give profound insights. All three planets are retrograde, so look to the past for guidance and inspiration. Cherished dreams and long-held ambitions will show you the way.

July

This is a month of endings. In the very first week, on Sunday 5, a full moon lunar eclipse in Capricorn brings something to a conclusion in your house of self and completes the Cancer-Capricorn eclipse series that began in 2018. During the past two years, this series has transformed your sense of who you are and how that reflects (and is reflected by) the important relationships in your life. Now it's all finished. There will be no more eclipses along this axis until 2027.

The final eclipse is very friendly, with Uranus, planet of change, and idealistic Neptune both in helpful angle, and with protective Jupiter close to the Moon. Whatever ends now, it's for the best. You may be in reflective mood, with retrograde Neptune closely involved and a lot of backwards-flowing energy focused on this axis. Make peace with the past, then let it go. This clears the way for wonderful new things to come into your life.

All the outer planets except Uranus are retrograde throughout the month, so there's a general sense of slowing down. It's a time for completion, or else for reviewing the past and using it to plan for the future. Projects may be put on hold, and delays interfere with your activities. Don't fight this. The time for action will come.

Just before the eclipse, on Thursday 2, Saturn retrogrades back into its home in Capricorn after a brief introductory visit to Aquarius and your money house. Issues you thought had been dealt with may surface again. This is a chance to make sure things are solid in all the areas that matter to you personally, and that you have truly learned all the lessons of Saturn's journey through your house of self.

Look back over the past three years to see what has changed for you. A little older and a lot wiser, you are now well placed to fix things in ways that last.

Saturn won't be back in Capricorn for many years, so do make sure you're on firm ground now. There won't be any further teaching until 2047. Happily, the knowledge you've gained will last until then.

Saturn will stay in Capricorn until December this year, so there is time to apply all you've learned. After that, though, the planet moves on. During the next few years, Saturn will be in Aquarius, testing your house of money and personal resources. Expect all sorts of issues and flaws to crop up in this area. It's all part of the process, so look forward with confidence.

On Sunday 12 Mercury turns direct in Cancer, your relationship house. There's always a bit of static in the air when a planet changes direction, so expect a flurry of glitches during the days surrounding this date. Mars and Uranus send fiery energy, so the atmosphere will be electric. Conflicts, arguments, and sudden upsets are likely. These may help clear the air, but hurt feelings are likely. Tread gently. Accidents and injuries are also possible, so be mindful of safety. Take good care of yourself and those around you, especially children.

On Monday 20 a new moon in Cancer brings a new beginning in this same house of relationships. The trouble is that Pluto, Saturn, and Jupiter all retrograde in direct opposition in Capricorn, your house of self, won't have any of it.

Most likely, you will be confronted by the possibility of unwelcome change in a relationship that matters to you. This can feel very threatening, so be kind to yourself (and to others!). Look for the positives if you can. Alternatively, you may want a change but come up hard against immovable obstacles. If so, you may feel held back, even shackled, by forces beyond your control. Either way, profound conflict is likely.

A new moon is usually a good time to start things, but anything you begin now will progress very slowly, if at all. Look deep within yourself to find out what you truly want to do. Is it important enough to brave all dangers for? If so, go ahead and act. But do listen to the voices raised in opposition. They may have a point. Make sure you've considered all the arguments against your new venture.

If you feel you need more time, a gorgeous new moon in Capricorn in January 2021 offers the perfect opportunity to act. All three outer planets will then be in happy support of the Moon. Use the intervening months to improve your plans! A further new moon in Cancer in June 2021 offers another possibility. Whatever your hopes, there's no need to rush into anything. You have lots of scope for preparation, before choosing a more favourable moment to launch.

There is another reason why delay might be preferable. On Wednesday 22 the Sun enters Leo, your house of shared property and inheritance, in direct opposition to Saturn, Pluto, and Jupiter all retrograde and clustered together in your own sun sign of Capricorn. Because the Sun rules Leo, it's at its strongest there. Expect major conflicts, power plays, and a massive showdown between ego demands on the one hand and mulish stubbornness on the other.

When an unstoppable force meets an immovable obstacle, the one place to avoid is the point of contact! Immense pressure will be brought to bear. Make sure you're not caught in the middle. If a confrontation is unavoidable, state your views clearly but don't try to force the issue. Hear the other person out.

Neptune in helpful angle appeals for calm. Look for common ground and the possibility of compromise. If none is possible, consider whether a delay would be in your own best interest. Building a watertight case now could bring you greater success next year.

August

Mars in Aries is a powerful thing. Friend or foe, this planet is the warrior of the zodiac. The one who conquers every obstacle, or gets the job done no matter what. This fierce passion is the reason why Mars rules fire sign Aries, and is at its strongest there.

Throughout this month, we feel the heat of Mars in its natural home in Aries, your house of home and family. Trouble is, Mars is slowing down and will turn retrograde next month. All that fiery energy is being held back, restrained, with nowhere to go.

What happens when an injured warrior can't fight? You guessed it. Combative planets, like competitive people, aren't always easy to be around.

But the glory of the zodiac is that nothing lasts forever. Mars will be back on its feet, hacking through any semblance of an enemy, before we know it.

Or, to be specific, after New Year. January 2021 will see Mars back to full strength. Until then, anything requiring courage in action will just have to wait.

Ouch. Does that mean we all have to sit on the sidelines for the second half of the year? Not a bit of it! We just have to box clever, and know our limitations.

You will feel the effects of the Mars retrograde most strongly in your domestic affairs, but the pent-up frustration and stalled energy will cause problems in other areas as well. Anything physical could be affected, so take care of your health and be mindful of safety. Avoid risks. Take extra care of any children in your life.

Angry confrontations and temperamental outbursts are likely. Take the high road if you can. Don't go toe to toe with anyone unless absolutely necessary. What begins as an argument could spiral into broken dishes, ruined relationships, and even violence.

Hard angles to powerful Pluto supported by protective Jupiter, both retrograde in your own sun sign of Capricorn, make the situation worse. Fierce conflicts could be unleashed this month. Old hurts and long-standing disagreements could erupt.

Saturn retrograde, also in your own sign, could uncover cracks in relationships or situations you thought were solid. Communicative Mercury opposite in sensitive Cancer, your relationship house, early in the month suggests that a showdown won't clear the air. You're more likely to say or hear things in the heat of the moment that can't be taken back or excused afterwards.

Everyone will feel this difficult energy. If you get the sense of having stepped into an alternate universe where everyone is unreasonable, rest assured it's not just you! Be patient with yourself and others. Things will improve eventually.

Although confrontations need careful handling, it's not a good time to seethe in silence. Say what needs to be said. Just choose your words with care.

Is there any good news at all? Well, Neptune in lovely angle does show a way of defusing the situation. Be the better person if you can. Consider the possibility that your opponent has a point, even if they express it badly. Treat obstacles and difficulties as a chance to improve, rather than as challenges to overcome.

With all this backwards-looking energy around, it's not a good time to start anything at all. Stick to existing projects and low-key work. Be open to feedback, and don't take things personally. Do what you can.

A difficult full moon in Aquarius on Monday 3 adds an unexpected broadside in your money house. Full moons bring endings, and with Uranus in hard angle this one may come as a shock. The warring planets in Aries and Capricorn aren't involved, but the tension between them makes for a combative atmosphere that won't help matters at all.

Tread with the utmost care. If things must change, accept this and make the best of it. Don't fight the inevitable. Accidents, injuries, and illness are possible, so be mindful of safety. Avoid risky activities. Keep a very close eye on any children in your life.

At mid-month, erratic Uranus turns retrograde, so expect plenty of static around this time. Unexpected events are likely, especially in your house of romance, children, and creative pursuits. Lovely angles to harmony planet Venus and protective Jupiter suggest a sudden turn of good fortune, so any disruption will be to your benefit.

During the next few weeks all the outer planets will be retrograde. Progress will slow to a crawl, especially on long-term projects. It's a time to look backwards rather than forwards. Review, restore, and re-consider. Don't press ahead or start anything completely new.

On Wednesday 19 a new moon in Leo signals the beginning of something in your house of shared property and inheritance. Action planet Mars in lovely angle in your house of home and family sends its frustrated energy your way. It's a great opportunity for a fresh take on anything that's been causing you problems, especially if other people are involved.

The next day, Thursday 20, Mercury enters Virgo, your house of travel and learning, which it rules. This is where the planet is strongest and happiest, so expect good things to follow. Shortly afterwards, the Sun moves into Virgo as well, shifting your focus firmly to this house. Mars continues to send all the energy it can muster, so this is a fabulous time to sort out anything that needs to be dealt with. With Uranus retrograde adding benevolent rays into the mix, good news and happy surprises are likely, perhaps involving your past.

Towards the end of the month, the stubborn outer planets in your own sun sign of Capricorn connect with Mercury. Hopeful messages may arrive regarding long-standing problems. Beautiful angles between the Sun and Mercury in Virgo, Uranus retrograde in Taurus, and Jupiter and Pluto both retrograde in Capricorn, show that the deadlock is at the point of being broken. These are all earth signs, so there won't be any headlong rush towards a solution, but clarity and sense are beginning to prevail.

An upcoming full moon in Pisces at the start of September will bring something to an end in your house of everyday routines (including your neighbourhood and workplace). Several of the difficult planets are involved, so it could be an excellent time to conclude the first round of talks. Stay positive!

September

Sunshine and showers best sums up the planetary forecast this month. Many different forces are in play, some harmonious and others the reverse! It's a confusing time, when some things will run smoothly and others snarl up into a hopeless mess. Pick your way through as best you can.

A full moon in Pisces on Wednesday 2 brings something to an end in your house of everyday routines. This is a happy full moon, with no less than three retrograde planets in support. Neptune, Jupiter, and Uranus all have blessings to share. Whatever happens is sure to delight you. It's an excellent time to finish up projects or visit familiar places. You may hear fabulous news.

At the same time, all is not well in the realm of relationships. Harmony planet Venus in sensitive Cancer is locked in conflict with the cluster of retrograde planets in your own sun sign of Capricorn. Strong emotions, frustration, and hurt feelings are likely. Almost everyone will notice these effects, so you are not alone! But it does make for a tense opening week.

The best thing to do is work patiently on long-term projects, keep a low profile, and avoid getting drawn into arguments. Let people have their way, if you can do so without compromising your principles. If you find yourself caught up in a swirl of emotion, put it down to the planetary influences and don't blame other people, especially your loved ones. Pretty much everyone is struggling right now.

With lots of retrograde energy around, it will be difficult to make headway on anything. Expect delays, obstacles, and flaws. Mars in Aries is slowing down, so all that fiery energy is being turned back on itself. Imagine a furnace at white heat! With Pluto and Saturn both retrograde and in hard angle, resentment could build to dangerous levels.

Be careful. Anything domestic is a tinderbox right now. One spark and it could all go up in flames. Accidents and injuries are possible, so be mindful of safety. Use extreme caution. Avoid risk.

On Wednesday 9 Mars turns retrograde in Aries, your house of home and family. Expect plenty of static in the days surrounding this date. With Venus, Pluto, and Saturn in hard angle, conflict and confrontation will be almost unavoidable. Try not to take anything personally.

Things are looking up in the world at large, though. Protective Jupiter in your own sun sign is in beautiful angle to other planets, and promises a change in the tide of fortune. On Sunday 13 Jupiter turns direct, still basking in planetary blessings. You'll probably feel the buzz in the air, so take note of any unusual events in the days surrounding this date. Good things are coming!

Just a few days later, on Thursday 17, a new moon in Virgo marks a new beginning in your travel house. This is a truly lovely new moon, with gorgeous angles to the troublesome three in your house of self. It's a fantastic time to push for a solution to recent problems. Jupiter is reaching out to planets all over the zodiac wheel in an effort to gather everyone around the table for fresh talks. Do use this positive energy to start working towards an agreement. It's also an excellent time to launch anything connected with travel or learning.

On Tuesday 22 the Sun moves into Libra, your career house. Venus, the ruler of Libra, is currently in Leo, which is ruled by the Sun. The two planets will amplify each other's positive energy, so everything connected with career and property is blessed right now. Bask in this summery warmth!

You may get further news concerning the spat between retrograde Mars in your house of home and family and the cluster of slow-moving planets in your own sun sign, as Mercury moves into the firing line. You probably won't like what you hear. But with Jupiter and Pluto now both in direct motion, and your ruler Saturn about to go direct at the end of the month, the tide is definitely turning. The Sun and Neptune both in helpful angle bring strength and patience to bear. Just keep on keepin' on. The happy ending is almost in sight.

Long-term projects that stalled under the retrograde outer planets could sputter back to life. Things will pick up in early October. You're not out of the woods yet, but there's every hope of getting back on the track.

New ventures and short-term projects will be heavy going for a few more weeks, as Mars continues retrograde until mid-November. Mercury retrograde will also throw a spanner in the works during that time. If you really must make a start on something, new moons in mid-November and mid-December offer good opportunities, but be prepared for significant delays, strong opposition, and major obstacles. It really is better to wait until next year if you can.

On Tuesday 29 your ruler Saturn goes direct in your own sign of Capricorn. Long-standing problems in your personal affairs are finally heading towards full resolution.

It may not feel like it at first, though. With Mars and Pluto both retrograde and at loggerheads, the situation may seem unsalvageable. Mercury in hard angle in your friendship house suggests bad news.

Old conflicts may resurface, especially involving people you care about. It's a cross and difficult time, with strong tensions between the planets.

Listen more than you speak. Strive to see beyond the surface. Idealistic Neptune in quiet talks with protective

Jupiter and powerful Pluto suggests a compromise may be possible. Look for common ground.

October

This will be a frustrating month. Mars continues retrograde in its home sign of Aries, your house of home and family, while picking fights with all three outer planets in Capricorn, your own sun sign and house of self. This could make things feel personal even when they're not. Conflicts, power struggles, and sullen anger may swirl around you, especially regarding people you care deeply about.

It's not easy to be a level-headed sun sign in a time of apparent crisis. Remember that you're fantastically well supported by planetary heavyweights. Your ruler Saturn, protective Jupiter, and powerful Pluto are all defending your turf. That's quite an alliance! Put your faith in the stars.

While Mars raises domestic concerns, Mercury sends static from your house of friendship (which includes groups, clubs, and organisations to which you belong). Glitches, delays, miscommunications, and misunderstandings will be rampant, especially at mid-month. Uranus in hard angle isn't helping, and will bring an element of the unpredictable. You may get bad news or experience sudden upsets.

On the very first day of the month, Thursday 1, a full moon in Aries brings something to an end in your house of home and family. With all this angry energy around, it's not a good time to do anything domestic unless you must. Let things happen in their own way. None of the other planets are involved with this full moon, so whatever ends now probably won't be too distressing for you. It's just a matter of rolling with the punches.

If you have projects to finish or matters to attend to, harmony planet Venus is sending soothing rays and will help you find a good conclusion. It's possible to get things settled under this full moon. Just avoid power struggles and angry confrontations. Be diplomatic. Seek a peaceful compromise to any disagreement.

Venus will spend the next couple of months moving through congenial Virgo and Libra, your houses of travel, learning, and career. This is a wonderful time to expand your horizons and pursue your ambitions. Love in all its forms will be blessed, so make a point of spending quality time with your dear ones.

A few days after the full moon, on Sunday 4, Pluto turns direct in your own sun sign of Capricorn. This means that all three outer planets that have caused so many headaches during the past few months are moving forward again. Finally things will pick up steam.

Mars retrograde in hard angle will take a while to come around, so expect problems and pushback in the domestic realm. But you are heading for a solution at last.

You may have a super day on or around Monday 5 as the Moon in Taurus receives joyful beams from the cluster of planets in your own sun sign of Capricorn. There's still a little bit of full-moon energy in the air, so anything that didn't quite happen for you last week can be brought to a happy conclusion now.

Move swiftly, because Saturday 10 will be an extremely difficult day, with angry cross-currents all over the chart. Do as little as possible in the days surrounding this date.

On Wednesday 14 Mercury turns retrograde in your friendship house. Expect a flurry of glitches in the days surrounding this date. Uranus retrograde in your house of love, opposite, will throw elements of the unexpected into the mix. Issues from the past may resurface. Gorgeous angles to Venus and Neptune suggest happy news, so this is likely to be a pleasant time overall. Prepare for minor snags, but laugh them off.

Enjoy the moment while it lasts. On Friday 16 an extremely difficult new moon in Libra sparks things off in your career house. This new moon speaks directly to the fierce battle between retrograde Mars in your house of home and family and the cluster of combative planets in your house of self. Their long conflict is heading for a showdown, and events under this new moon will set the stage.

Do as little as possible. Harmonious Venus is sending messages of love and peace throughout the zodiac wheel from your house of travel and learning, so view all this upset as an opportunity to grow. Doors are opening for you, even if all you can hear is the sound of angry voices.

If you have projects to get off the ground, launch in mid-November or mid-December for best effect. Don't go all out right now. It's a time for patient, low-key work, detailed planning and careful reviews.

On Thursday 22 the Sun moves into Scorpio, riding to the rescue of embattled Mercury in your friendship house. Uranus retrograde in your house of love, opposite, causes all sorts of issues to bubble up. Delve deep and strive for clarity on what the real problem might be.

It's a time for looking backwards rather than forwards. Face the past with courage and honesty. Then you will know what to do.

On Saturday 31 a full moon in Taurus brings the issue into sharp focus. The mighty Sun in your friendship house opposes the sensitive Moon and erratic Uranus in your house of love. You may feel stymied and frustrated in the days surrounding this date. What you want may not be possible, or you may resist the demands of other people. Something will end in your house of love under this full moon, and it may not make you happy. Take heart! Venus, the ruler of this house, is well aspected in fair-minded Libra, and this will help things turn out for the best.

Usually a full moon is a good time to finish things, but you may find it difficult to get your own way right now. Be open to alternatives. It may be worth waiting a day or two before making your move. If you can afford to delay matters for a few weeks more, you may find it easier to resolve things to your own satisfaction at the end of November, when aspects are more favourable. Until then, just do your best.

November

This is a month of two halves. The first two weeks are taken up with the Mars and Mercury retrogrades, which stall progress and snarl up even the most innocuous activities. Don't expect to get far during this time, especially with new ventures or short-term projects.

On the plus side, harmonious Venus in fair-minded Libra, which it rules, soothes and pacifies relationships in general. Idealistic Neptune in dreamy Pisces sends blessings all around the chart. That's just as well, because all the other planets are at loggerheads as the month opens. Hard angles and relentless standoffs make this a time of deep frustration, conflict, and anger.

You will feel the effects most strongly in the realm of home and family, but with so many planets involved there will be problems everywhere. It may seem as if you just can't get ahead, no matter what you do. That's probably true right now, so don't push. Listen more than you speak. Review your situation, and pay special attention to any flaws or difficulties that come up. Use this knowledge to improve your plans for the future. Act on them under the new moon at mid-month or in December, or else save them for next year. They'll keep.

The first week of the month will be especially frazzled as Mercury changes direction on Tuesday 3. Expect a lot of static on this day. All sorts of snags and glitches are likely. The effects will be strongest in the professional arena, but every part of your life may be affected. This may seem overwhelming, but keep your chin up. It's better to know the truth. The Moon in helpful angle suggests you may even feel relieved to get some answers. Stay positive!

On Tuesday 10 Mercury moves into Scorpio, your friendship house, and comes under fire from heavyweights Saturn and Uranus. Bad news, unwelcome surprises, sharp criticism and hostile encounters are all possible around this time. Don't take any of it to heart. The Sun in the same sign is basking in joyful beams from Pluto and Neptune, so your outlook is excellent. Use whatever problems come to light as a source of information. Towards the end of the month, aspects will be ideal for resolving them.

For now, keep a low profile. Mid-month will be a difficult time. Aggressive Mars changes direction on Saturday 14 in your house of home and family, while in hard angle to powerful Pluto in your house of self. Expect fireworks! Angry outbursts, fierce conflicts, power struggles and domineering behaviour are likely in the days surrounding this date. Don't get drawn into hostilities. Be mindful of safety. Avoid risk.

On Sunday 15 a new moon in Scorpio signals the beginning of something in your friendship house. This is a beautiful moon, with lovely angles to Neptune in your house of everyday routines (including your neighbourhood and workplace) and the cluster of planets in your own sun sign and house of self. At last things are looking up!

In the days following this new moon, you'll feel a breath of fresh air sweeping through your life. It's an excellent time to start projects of all kinds, especially if they involve other people or long-standing plans. Hold off on anything domestic for now, though, as Mars hasn't got up to speed yet.

Mercury will remain sluggish until late in the month, and Mars until the New Year, so we're not out of the woods yet. But the next few weeks will be a lot easier. Enjoy!

It's an especially good time to press on with anything that matters to you personally, since Saturn and Jupiter are spending their final weeks in your own sun sign of Capricorn before moving on in mid-December. Don't expect instant results, but do make every effort to achieve your goals. Mars will continue to object in your house of home and family, but its opposition will gradually weaken and eventually disappear in January 2021. It's time for the big finish. Stay strong!

On Saturday 21 the Sun moves into Sagittarius and lights up the area of inner needs and the unconscious. Jupiter, the ruler of Sagittarius, is in full direct motion and in happy angle to the Sun, so there's lots of energy available for whatever you wish to do during the coming weeks. Anything that matters deeply to you will be blessed!

Monday 23 will be a superb day for anything involving other people, as the Moon close to Neptune retrograde in Pisces receives a shower of blessings from planets in Scorpio and Capricorn. You may hear fabulous news or enjoy a magical time with people you care about.

If you celebrate Christmas or any other holiday at this time of year, make your preparations now. Aspects are ideal.

On Sunday 29 Neptune turns direct in your house of everyday routines, which it rules. Happy beams from other planets add to the positive energy. Take note of anything that comes up.

Right at the end of the month, on Monday 30, a full moon lunar eclipse in Gemini brings something to an end in your house of health and work. This is the second eclipse in the Gemini-Sagittarius series that began in June. Then, something ended in your house of inner needs (which includes your hopes, aims, and ambitions). Now, something will end in your house of health and work, where your actions in pursuit of those needs take physical form. Throughout next year, this series will continue to overhaul your houses of inner needs and outer health, what you want and how you go about achieving it, ending in December 2021 with the start of a fresh chapter in your house of inner needs.

The current eclipse is very friendly. No planets are involved other than the Sun and Moon, so you may encounter a straightforward conclusion to something that is no longer relevant to your life.

Mercury, the ruler of Gemini, is in happy talks with Jupiter, the ruler of Sagittarius, while both planets are in full forward motion and beautifully aspected. This promises wonderful new developments in the aftermath of this eclipse. You may get excellent news, bringing extra sparkle to a satisfying conclusion.

It's generally best not to start anything under the influence of an eclipse, since events move rapidly and circumstances can change without warning. Also, a full moon is a time of endings rather than beginnings, so it's better to wrap things up than start afresh. But if you see the opportunity to respond to a promising lead, or put existing plans in motion, this could be a suitable moment. There's so much positive energy around that you can't go far wrong.

Other than that, your attention is best focused on tying up loose ends and making sure everything is done and dusted.

Out with the old! The solar eclipses next month and during 2021 will take care of bringing in the new.

December

This is the month when everything brightens. The glow of last month's eclipse lights up the first week, with truly lovely aspects between the planets. All that positive energy is flowing freely around the personal section of the chart, so everything you do is blessed! Even Mars is beginning to come around, strengthened by a supportive Sun. Fire brings both heat and light, so expect some flashes within the growing brilliance. But mostly these opening weeks will be positive and uplifting. If you celebrate Christmas or any other holiday at this time of year, enjoy the party spirit!

Mars is now direct in Aries but still a little groggy from its recent retrograde. It's not an ideal time to start brand new projects, especially on the domestic front. Wait until the new year if you can. But if you have minor matters to kick into gear, or want to get things sorted out before Christmas, there is plenty of planetary support.

Only Uranus in Taurus is hitting the brakes, being retrograde in your house of love. Venus, the ruler of Taurus, is in direct opposition in Scorpio, your friendship house. Whatever your aims and plans regarding loved ones, creative pursuits, or anything you're passionate about, now is not the time to force them through. You may feel held back by the demands of other people or by your own hesitation, but either way things just aren't happening.

Let it go for now. A new moon in Taurus in May next year will give you the perfect opportunity to act. After that, we are heading for a new series of eclipses on the Taurus-Scorpio axis, which will shake things up in your houses of love and friendship. Whatever you do in these areas during the next few months will be subject to change in any case, so don't worry too much about it. Enjoy the positive energy that centres on you personally instead.

Venus in Scorpio will quickly reward your patience. Saturday 12 is a magical day for your social life, as Venus escapes from the erratic influence of Uranus and basks in the loving support of almost all the other planets. Everything connected with friendship will be blessed. Don't try to do too much, as the next eclipse is upon us, but enjoy all the happy rays beaming down on you.

On Monday 14 a new moon solar eclipse in Sagittarius opens a new chapter in your house of inner needs. This continues the Gemini-Sagittarius series that started last June. The current eclipse is all fire and flame, with the Sun and Mars both in congenial fire signs and in gorgeous angle. Expect your world to be set alight!

Take care not to get singed, though. Mercury in close support brings clarity to the situation, but Neptune in hard angle covers it in a fog of confusion. It may not be easy to get your bearings, even if you think you know exactly where you are. Don't blunder into the fire by mistake. Scrutinise everything carefully.

As you know, it's always best not to start anything under an eclipse. Events move rapidly, and circumstances can change in the blink of an eye. But if you've had to put existing plans on hold because of delays over the past few months, the energy of this eclipse will breathe new life into them. Press on if you

·

feel it's right to do so, but move with caution. If you can wait a few days, Friday 18 is a better time to act. The worst frazzle will be over by then, and splendid aspects will give you every chance of success.

On Tuesday 15 Venus enters Sagittarius, still receiving lovely beams from Jupiter, the ruler of that sign. Saturn adds its voice in a final blessing from its home in your own sign of Capricorn. You may find good things already following in the wake of the eclipse.

This is the end of Saturn's three-year journey through Capricorn. On Thursday 17 the planet moves into Aquarius, your money house. Expect to uncover all sorts of flaws and problems regarding money and other personal resources in the next few years. Remember that Saturn's mission is to help us improve, so do embrace this opportunity to learn and grow.

Uranus, the ruler of Aquarius, remains in hard angle and may start raising issues immediately. These will probably relate to the past, since Uranus is retrograde, and may involve your house of love as well. Don't expect to find solutions right away. Both planets are slow-moving, and with Uranus retrograde you may feel as if you're treading water or even going backwards. Be patient. Things will start to move in the right direction during early 2021, but it may take a year or more to resolve the situation in full. You have plenty of time to put your finances in order.

On Saturday 19 Jupiter follows Saturn into Aquarius, adding strength to that side of the tug of war. Only Pluto remains in Capricorn, where it will continue for many years to come.

This marks the beginning of the end of the tussle between Mars in Aries and the cluster of planets in Capricorn. With the Sun and Mercury travelling together in fire sign Sagittarius and sending supportive rays to Mars, things will be charging ahead in your house of home and family. If you have things to accomplish, especially domestic matters, now is an excellent time.

On Monday 21 the Sun moves into your own sun sign of Capricorn, with speedy Mercury having done so the previous day. This marks the beginning of your birthday month, and will set the tone for the year that follows. You have splendid aspects, so expect wonderful things! Great news may arrive out of the blue. If you have projects to launch, aim to get them off the ground in mid-January when a fabulous new moon in Capricorn will give you fantastic support.

It's a good time for travel, so head off for that Christmas break with confidence. The holidays themselves look happy and peaceful, with wonderful aspects relating to health, loved ones, travel, neighbourhood, and friends.

That said, Mars in your house of home and family is in angry altercation with Saturn in your money house. Unwelcome expenses, quarrels over money, and domestic tensions of all kinds seem possible. You may prefer to duck out of duty visits, steer clear of discussions about money, and brace for cashflow problems. Be cautious in your spending. Avoid arguments if you can.

New Year will be a little unsettled. A full moon in Cancer on Wednesday 30 brings something to an end in your relationship house. Uranus retrograde in happy angle throws an element of the unexpected into the mix, perhaps related to the past. At the same time, your ruler Saturn in Aquarius in hard angle to Uranus, the ruler of that sign, suggests that something may break irretrievably at this time.

You may get a pleasant surprise or come to a startling conclusion, but discover that this puts the final nail in the coffin of a situation that hasn't been working out. Let it be so. Whatever passes from your life now will set you free. Head into 2021 with a spring in your step, ready for all the excitement the future has to offer.

The Year Ahead: 2021

This is a year of upheaval. Stern Saturn in Aquarius will be locked in conflict with rebellious Uranus in Taurus throughout this year and the next. That creates enormous tension between your houses of money and love. You may feel trapped, frustrated, and held back by rigid constraints. Perhaps you struggle to satisfy the demands of your loved ones, or else your desires are stymied by the limits of your purse. Either way, you lack the resources to support the needs of the heart.

Don't expect any quick fixes. Both these planets are slow-moving, and the hard angle between them won't disappear until 2022, so you'll be dealing with difficult issues for some time.

Take a good long look at these areas of your life. Are they all that you want them to be? The upsets, obstacles, and confrontations that occur may be telling you something. Perhaps it's time for a change.

On the plus side, Neptune and Pluto continue their happy relationship, creating peace and understanding throughout your everyday life. It's a wonderful time to connect with your ordinary environment, whether through friends and neighbours or involvement in local activities, and to make sure your lifestyle reflects your highest ideals. By living true to yourself, you'll manifest more fully your own chosen destiny.

Jupiter in Aquarius will magnify the opportunities that come with disruption, especially in your house of money and personal resources. Be open to possibilities, and you'll reap rich rewards.

The Gemini-Sagittarius eclipse series that began in 2020 continues during early summer and ends with a solar eclipse in Sagittarius in early December. This concludes the transformation the series has brought to your houses of inner needs and outer health, what you want and how you go about achieving it. There will be no more eclipses on the Gemini-Sagittarius axis until 2029.

A new eclipse series starts on the Taurus-Scorpio axis towards the end of the year, with a lunar eclipse in Taurus in mid-November. This will add to the upheaval in your house of love, so expect the unexpected! The series will transform the areas of love and friendship for you, concluding with a lunar eclipse in Taurus during late October 2023.

Also towards the end of the year, Venus will turn retrograde in your own sun sign of Capricorn, your solar house of self. With plenty of other planets rallying around in support, this isn't likely to be troublesome. It's a time to slow down and enjoy all the blessings of your personal life. Venus rules your houses of love and career, so connect with the people and projects that matter most to you. Dust off those dreams, and reach for the stars!

***

FREQUENTLY ASKED QUESTIONS

Question: I know my Ascendant (Rising Sign) and Moon Sign. Should I read for those as well?

Answer: You can if you want to, but there's no need. The Ascendant or Rising Sign shows your outlook on life and what you tend to manifest naturally. The Moon Sign shows your emotional landscape and how you tend to react to events. But the Sun Sign shows your sense of self, who you are and what you choose to do. The forecasts are designed to help you plan and execute your own decisions, so the Sun Sign forecast is completely sufficient.

Question: I worry about difficult aspects coming up. Help!

Answer: These can be stressful. Think of them as dammed-up energy. With care, it can be used to good effect. Trust yourself to find a way through. You're stronger than you think!

Question: I can't always time my actions the way you suggest. Is it OK to ignore your advice and do my own thing?

Answer: Absolutely! Always use your own best judgement. You are the expert on your life and circumstances. Also, do remember that we're all fallible. Astrologers can be wrong, too!

Question: I'd like a detailed individual forecast. Are you taking new clients?

Answer: Unfortunately, no.

QUICK GUIDE TO THE HOROSCOPE

A horoscope is a map of the heavens, showing the location of the planets as seen from the Earth. It is divided into twelve sections named after star constellations, known as the signs of the zodiac. The Sun and Moon count as planets, as does Pluto.

The sign in which the Sun was located at the moment of your birth is of huge importance in shaping your fundamental nature and your outlook on life. This is known as your sun sign. Many people who aren't familiar with their full birth horoscope only know their sun sign, so they often refer to it in a shorthand way as their star sign.

In fact, the sun sign only represents one key aspect of your astrological personality: your conscious self. The other eleven signs also represent important areas of lived experience. All twelve zodiac signs taken together, counting from the sun sign, are known as the solar houses.

By knowing which planets will be in a certain house, and in what angle to other planets in other houses, we can predict the influence they are likely to have in various areas of your life.

Without a detailed individual birth horoscope, as well as knowledge of your personal circumstances, it is not possible for anyone else to predict the exact events you will experience. But you are the expert on your own life! Read the forecasts, and consider how they apply to your specific situation. Then plan accordingly, and be amazed at the results.

***

ABOUT THE AUTHOR

Zoe Buckden has been an astrologer in private practice for almost thirty years. She lives in the north of England with several cats and the occasional hedgehog.

ABOUT BYRNIE PUBLISHING

We are a small independent publisher specialising in genre fiction and popular nonfiction.

Made in the USA
Columbia, SC
20 December 2019

85495464R00062